Hard Work

A Day with a Carpenter

By Joanne Winne

Children's Press
A Division of Grolier Publishing
New York / London / Hong Kong / Sydney
Danbury, Connecticut

Photo Credits: Cover and all photos by Maura Boruchow
Contributing Editor: Jeri Cipriano
Book Design: Michael DeLisio

Visit Children's Press on the Internet at:
http://publishing.grolier.com

Library of Congress Cataloging-in-Publication Data

Winne, Joanne.
  A day with a carpenter / by Joanne Winne.
   p. cm. (Hard work)
  Includes bibliographical references and index.
  ISBN 0-516-23136-7 (lib. bdg.) — ISBN 0-516-23061-1 (pbk.)
  1. Carpentry—Vocational guidance—Juvenile literature. 2. Carpenters—Juvenile
literature. [1. Carpenters. 2. Occupations.] I. Title. II. Series.

TH5068.8 .W55 2000
694'.023—dc21

                                                        00-034569

Contents

My name is John.

I am a **carpenter**.

5

I use wood to build things.

Today, I am building
a **bench**.

7

I wear gloves on my hands.

I wear boots on my feet.

I wear a belt that holds my tools.

9

I wear special glasses.

The glasses **protect** my eyes.

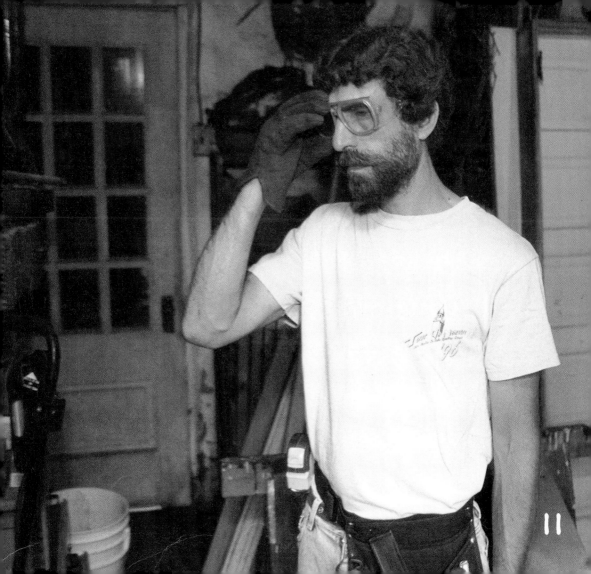

11

I use a **ruler**.

I **measure** the wood
with the ruler.

13

I use a saw to cut the wood.

15

I use a **hammer** to **pound nails** into the wood.

The nails hold together the pieces of wood.

17

I rub the bench with **sandpaper**.

Sandpaper makes the wood **smooth**.

19

Now the bench is done.

Tomorrow, I will build
a chair.

I like being a carpenter.

21

New Words

bench (**bench**) a long seat

carpenter (**kar**-pen-ter) a person who builds
   things made of wood

hammer (**ham**-er) a tool used to hit nails

measure (**mezh**-er) to find out how long or
   wide something is

nails (**naylz**) thin pieces of metal used to hold
   together two pieces of wood

pound (**pownd**) to hit

protect (proh-**tekt**) to keep safe

ruler (**roo**-ler) something used to measure

sandpaper (**sand**-pay-per) paper with sand
   glued onto it; it is used to smooth wood

smooth (**smooth**) even, with no bumps

To Find Out More

Books
Bruno the Carpenter
by Lars Klinting
Henry Holt & Company

Carpenter
by Angela McHanley Brown
Raintree Steck-Vaughn

Web Site
What Do They Do: Carpenter
http://www.whatdotheydo.com/carpentr.htm
You can read about what carpenters do and the tools that they use on this Web site.

Index

bench,
   6, 18, 20

carpenter,
   4, 20

hammer, 16

measure, 12

nails, 16

pound, 16
protect, 10

ruler, 12

sandpaper, 18
smooth, 18

About the Author

Joanne Winne taught fourth grade for nine years. She currently writes and edits books for children. She lives in Hoboken, New Jersey.

Reading Consultants

Kris Flynn, Coordinator, Small School District Literacy, The San Diego County Office of Education

Shelly Forys, Certified Reading Recovery Specialist, W.J. Zahnow Elementary School, Waterloo, IL

Peggy McNamara, Professor, Bank Street College of Education, Reading and Literacy Program